THREE HUNDRED AND TWENTY-ONE

HAIKU

INTIMATE REFLECTIONS

MICHAEL J. LEE

© Michael J. Lee 2020

First Edition 2020

The right of Michael J. Lee to be identified as the author of this book has been asserted in accordance with the Copyright, Designs and Patents Act 1988.

All rights reserved. No part of this publication may be reproduced, distributed or transmitted in any form or by any means, including photocopying, recording, or other electronic or mechanical methods, without the prior written permission of the publisher, except in the case of brief quotations embodied in critical reviews and certain other noncommercial uses permitted by copyright law.

For permission requests, write to the publisher, addressed "Attention: Permissions Coordinator," at michael@positivedestiny.org.

ISBN 978-1-990957-65-9 (eBook)

ISBN 978-1-990957-69-7 (Print)

www.michaeljlee.com

www.beyondheads.com

Cover and interior crafted with love by the team at:
www.myebook.online

Contents

Poet's Preface

You may ask, why 321 haiku in this collection? In reverse, this number reads as 123. When we say, "easy as 123", we indicate simplicity. Simplicity involves distilling the essence of an idea, insight or observation. The aim of a haiku is to highlight some of the power and beauty in nature's underlying simplicity. We see this commitment to a kind of minimalism both in the small size of the poem and in its strict order.

Another defining characteristic of haiku is counting syllables: 5 in the first line, 7 in the second line and then cyclically back to 5 in the last line. There's an obvious numeric dimension in the 5-7-5 structure. Perhaps the Japanese pioneers of this ancient kind of poetry were intuitively conscious, like some Ancient Greek thinkers, of the mathematical foundation behind nature. The laws of gravity and motion, and the precision of planetary orbits, would later confirm this reality through scientific observation and mathematical calculation.

Despite there being this strong order compacted into a short space, haiku should remain personal. I originally wanted to call this collection of poems *Through My Eyes*, but that sounded too egotistical for verses looking to combine personal reflections with universal themes. Nevertheless, the volume's overall tone is intimate and even spiritual. I tried to capture brief experiences and thoughts in instants of time.

Finally, in this Internet Age we're in, concise expressions will always work better than over-elaborate descriptions, and so it's hoped there'll be a long life ahead for a form of poetry which can be enjoyed in an instant.

Michael Lee

Cape Town

2020

1. Thought

God is like the thought
in which all things were conceived:
laws of nature rule.

2. Rising

As morning rises
first birds, then machines, then me:
drowsy with darkness.

3. New Year's Eve Sunset

Gale batters beach palms,
waves thrashing tidal pool walls:
a pinpoint Sun sets.

4. Change

Daily grind and dreams
like a cobweb in suspense
blowing away soon.

5. Big Birth

Power boom; big bang,
a universe explosion;
emerging order.

6. Hard Rain

Birds and trees don't doubt,
feeling the hard rain falling;
soon, the drought will end.

7. Air

Yes, winter is here,
yes, crisp and clear is the air:
yes, a mountain breeze.

8. Orbital

Lunar orbited
Earth rotates a snowy peak:
moon lightens the dome.

9. Wife

My wife, my friend, we
travel together at peace,
accepting our fate.

10. Sleepy Peace

How wholly pleasant
to fall asleep reading verse:
drugged by deep peace.

11. More Peace

What you have or find
on a lonely day is peace
you can carry home.

12. Seekers

Like cats seek out heat
our spirits search this wide world
for security.

13.   Order

Underpinning all
is God's fixed solar order,
timeless in aeons.

14.   Awake

Little twitters spark,
speckled light behind curtains,
engine in the sky.

15.   Immaculate

Immaculate light
once spoken into being:
travels forever.

16. *Demons*

Beat hard the demons
before they smother your heart:
rise up, clean and free.

17. *Three Times*

Living in three worlds,
the present, past and future,
I chase destiny.

18. *Revolt of a Man*

I now find myself
a rebel against the world
in which phonies win.

19. *Happiness*

Old, I am searching,
but there's just one happiness:
the one you have found.

20. *Weather*

Cold front, warm clothing,
grey skies, dreaming of sunlight,
between now and then.

21. *Tools*

Taps, basin, toilet,
oven, fridge, fork, spoon, clothes, desk:
tools of living well.

22.   *First Light*

Before first light broke
the water was cold and dark:
a womb in waiting.

23.   *Bad Dream*

Traces of a dream
from some deep cave in my mind:
ignored at daybreak.

24.   *On the Run*

Am I far away
by design or by default?
Run with destiny!

25.   Origin

In the Origin
a spirit hovered over
the shapeless darkness.

26.   Early Sounds

Bird talk breaks silence,
then long rays of sun bring noise:
cars and a lone plane.

27.   60/40 Vision

Manage your present,
imagineer future time:
as sixty/forty?

28. *Lights*

Torches in the night,
stars shine perfection on us,
colouring this world.

29. *In Alignment*

Rhythms of the day
slow down under silent stars
eternally placed.

30. *Rule*

Light and colour rule,
star-fires birthed elements,
a cosmos was made.

31.   *Mother City*

City of colour,
contradictions, character:
cosmopolitan.

32.   *One Night*

Midnight, wide awake,
full of memories, questions:
pray for tomorrow.

33.   *Imagination*

Fix eyes on high things
of timeless significance:
eternal faces.

34. Gender

In the gender war
who will manipulate whom?
The one who loves self.

35. Self-Belief

Believe in yourself,
belief will bring you relief.
God believes in you.

36. Beauty

The cosmic beauty
gives me hope for our future:
creation triumphs.

37. Aspire Higher

Let go, Boy, let go,
let's go into a new time,
free from past causes.

38. Shapes

The world looks better
through the eyes of kindliness:
hate's misshapen dreams.

39. Living Inside

In a thinking box,
in a country within worlds
I live in my home.

40.   *Fearless*

Bold is believing,
unafraid of future, past
or our enemies.

41.   *Fears*

Fears float like bad dreams
in a dark world of powers:
resist thought control.

42.   *My Wife*

True to me is she,
free from pretension or guile,
my time-traveller.

43.   Rabbit

Wild white rabbit hops
woolly on the cool green grass
nibbling its breakfast.

44.   Good?

Believe in goodness,
trust in a higher power:
let negatives go.

45.   Goodness

Goodness goes with God.
I base actions on manners,
directing my ways.

46. Crabs

Like a hermit crab,
I'm only as good as home:
I seek a strong shell.

47. Letting Go

Like a pruned rosebush
I let all memories go:
bring on my new growth!

48. Pia Mater

All you could and had
you gave us, gentle as air,
quietly as light.

49. Bird

Little yellow bird
without any tools or pay
pecking lavender.

50. Arise

Behind the curtains,
beyond blinds, windows and walls,
rises a lone sun.

51. Skins

As a snake sheds skin
I'm as good as my last work:
seeking a new form.

52.   Anger, Hate, Rage

We know: let hate go.
Anger destroys peace and lives.
We know: let rage go.

53.   The Offer

I take his offer
on the cross to forgive me
freely and fully.

54.   In Contention

I count all I have,
counterbalancing dark thoughts:
let me live strongly.

55.   Writer

If I'm a writer,
who am I with no new words
or stories to tell?

56.   Worlds

The old world is gone
and I no longer belong:
steel cool, stone cold world.

57.   Powers

You'd need to be God
to count stars or slow down tides
or make waterfalls.

58. *Self-Interest*

Self-interest rules
but it's not okay like this,
it breaks everything.

59. *A Definition*

By definition
God would be the greatest force
there has ever been.

60. *Astronomic*

I see a picture
without a frame of our home
without end or walls.

61. *Choices*

Choose kindness, not rage,
helpfulness not aggression;
wish a stranger well.

62. *Safe*

I'm safe in the dark
like a blind man feels his way
early each morning.

63. *Artist*

If I'm an artist...
who am I with no vision
and no world to draw?

---

64.   *Melkbos Calling*

Sweet sunshine cascades
on the bay of sand and surf,
its waves rolling on.

65.   *Return to Sender*

This world you gave me,
with chains of cause-and-effect,
I return to you.

66.   *Trumpism*

News blurts out slogans,
vulgar populists sell hate:
untrue, twisted, mean.

67.   *Federer*

Cool ambassador,
his gentle soul-fire burns,
destroying defeat.

68.   *Balance (1)*

It wasn't given,
it was chiselled from marble:
equilibrium.

69.   *5/7/5*

First line is right hand,
then comes the perfect number,
third is my left hand.

---

70. Future

Who steals my future?
Who obstructs my destiny?
God decides my times.

71. Escape

Escape into God,
escape into art, love, truth:
anywhere but here.

72. Sequel

I plan a sequel
to life about the future:
immortality.

73. Journey

The journey is on
to find out why I'm alive,
to travel in peace.

74. Sin too Far

The one sin too far
is wasting life with bad deeds:
only goodness lives.

75. Active

Challenges, problems,
disappointments, frustrations:
let me pray and plan.

76.   *Imagine*

How long does it take
to discover who you are?
An imagineer!

77.   *Winter's Day*

Bone cold storm erupts
churning low skies of Cape Town:
huddling together.

78.   *Homebound*

How far to my home?
The distance between nowhere
and this everywhere.

79.   *Greatness*

Thank you for your grace.
Thank you for your true greatness.
Thanks for being God.

80.   *Road*

Alone was I, once,
when God saw me on the road,
showing me his home.

81.   *Bees*

Bees without money
busy in the purple bush
producing goodness.

82.   *Universe*

May I be worthy,
sailing in a strong boat, on
seas without a shore.

83.   *Loneliness*

Is my loneliness
the only cure I will find
for being alone?

84.   *Almost*

Almost broken up,
seeking comforts, seeking peace:
God, my final hope.

85. *Loved*

I am not afraid
every time you are near me:
encompassed by love.

86. *Brief Words*

Unshaven and calm,
a haiku popped in my head
as I brushed my teeth.

87. *Stem Cell Transplant*

A second chance dawned,
new blood, new life transplanted:
leukaemia washed!

88.   *Purer*

Forget not to ask,
as night falls, for forgiveness –
for each pollution.

89.   *Cosmic Viewpoint*

Teaching unlearns me,
my life isn't about me,
clad in cosmic awe.

90.   *Calls*

An open window
lets the world in as I wake:
get up, rise with us.

91. *Voyage*

The long journey home
is a space-time adventure:
Father, make me brave.

92. *Cohesive*

God of cohesion,
forever keep me as one
in your timeless name.

93. *Waking*

Awake with machines,
trucks, trains, motor cars and planes,
the city inside.

94. Free

Not in hate but love
I live, nor in cold revenge:
Let go: past of pain.

95. Three Worlds

Digital era,
physical world, God's kingdom:
intersecting me.

96. Unselfish

Selfish is easy.
Empathy is a duty.
Or a ministry.

97.   *Limbo*

In limbo was I,
an unknown, unsure of love,
until love found me.

98.   *Face*

Feeling a bit down?
Trick your face with a quick smile;
re-booting your mind.

99.   *Humble*

Humble I remain
before an almighty throne
and awestruck cosmos.

100. *Free*

Free thought: comforting.
"Cogito ergo sum" rules.
I think for myself.

101. *Strong*

Dread became a fear.
Then I fought the fear with faith:
my spirit stronger.

102. *Opportunity*

Not a silhouette,
not a shadow or omen:
optimise real life.

103. True

I'll be true to you,
you give me light and water;
and all in-between.

104. Longing

Born for love, I longed
day and night for its true source,
until God found me.

105. Healers

Healing makes us strong,
Searching science and God's face
to cure what's gone wrong.

106. Another God Haiku

Daily I love God,
God loves like I'm family:
who else dies for me?

107. Evolution

First published in *Stanzas* poetry magazine

All the fears and
tears of our million years
vibrate in my brain.

108. Love Verse

I love Love, just as
Love loves me...like family:
who else cares for me?

109. *Time Out*

First published in *Stanzas* poetry magazine

Onboard, you don't know
how fast the train is going:
only onlookers.

110. *Empty and Full*

Empty me of all –
illusions and pretensions –
but love from above.

111. *Alive*

Organisms in
their ecosystem: within
one bright biosphere.

112. Once

I'm here once only,
too many flaws and failures:
love is victory.

113. Aborigines

Where have they all gone,
the land's originals?
Why have you hurt them?

114. Ghosts of An Undying Past

We weep for hurts caused,
for open wounds, divisions:
we pray for wholeness.

115. God

No love is wasted
on God, whose light is constant,
whose forces hold firm.

116. Orientation

Dawn opens our dome,
face God, turn, orientate:
gain good direction.

117. Hands

Work lightly with hands,
carry, construct, cut, create:
labouring dearly.

118.   *Established*

As for all nature,
I am established in truth,
unshakeably firm.

119.   *Sunny Sky*

The Sun is my friend,
it powers me up, heals me:
my high orb of hope.

120.   *Mystic sleep*

Like a monastery
is sleep, still, deep and sacred,
a pool of oneness.

121.   Adventure

Soaking in sunlight,
waiting for hours to pass:
life is adventure.

122.   Under the Wave off Kanagawa

(in honour of Hokusai)

One still high white point
beyond boats beating the sea
exploding water.

123.   Waters

Deep, dark waters flowed.
Then water was divided:
skies, aquifers, seas.

124. Southern Cross

Tall palm leaves shield stars
nailed to a cross in the sky:
grey-blue winter night.

125. Lowest Point

At the lowest point,
between her fear and despair,
the healer is there.

126. Reboot

Switch on your own mind,
clear your conscience of bad deeds,
reboot your power.

127. Attraction

The Milky Way's laws
give the earth security:
held in gravity.

128. The Kiss

In the street they kiss;
isn't love just beautiful,
creating our world?

129. Only

Only God knows all,
only God lives forever,
only grace is good.

130. Lonely Boy

The boy was a man.
He became a child of God,
being first loved then.

131. Res Gesta Per Excellentiam

NASA kissed the stars,
sailed through the solar system;
now, go get us Mars.

132. Rain

Morning breaks in peace,
the poetry is raining:
dripping gently home.

133. Autumn Morning

Tapestry of trees,
hazy mountain in blue air:
fresh grass and ground cools.

134. Promises, Pontifications and Platitudes

Politics, power,
their price we pay is too high:
seek the timeless way.

135. Two Cats

Our two cats, sisters,
were kittens once in our palms,
becoming soul-friends.

136. Eternal Family

Undeservedly,
eternally, God loves me:
a family tree.

137. Old Time

Time is an old tree,
roots in the ground of the past:
futures will flower.

138. Reorientation

Switch God on inside,
turn love up, open your eyes,
look outwards: see all.

139. Cats

On an empty day
two cats lay asleep indoors,
their fur curled inward.

140. True

I'll be true to you,
you give me light and water;
greatly you give, God.

141. Listening

Hear your body talk
but don't believe everything
it wants to tell you.

142. *Morning 1*

First published in *Stanzas* poetry magazine

Kingfisher sparkles
on first opening roses;
outside is inside.

143. *Morning 2*

First published in *Stanzas* poetry magazine

Fresh drizzle at dawn,
father and daughter cycling:
their tyres sizzle.

144. *Morning 3*

First published in *Stanzas* poetry magazine

Sings the glad, green ground:
fist of red geranium
shakes our status quo.

---

145. *Morning 4*

First published in *Stanzas* poetry magazine

The wet drips around
soaking surrounds in promise
while a peacock sulks.

146. *Morning 5*

Drizzled hush of drops,
somewhere a mother goose quacks;
feel Africa feed.

147. *Balls*

Novak Djokovic
plays his heart out on the court;
to vanquish with love.

____

148. Kind

Look on the kind side,
it's there under scars on skin
and bleeding spirits.

149. Rain Again

Water falling hard,
art without architecture:
an excited earth.

150. Margin for Error

Failure's stepping stones
take me closer to success;
I'm not my mistakes.

151.   The Clash

Insurmountable.
Invincible. Who will win?
Believe for the best.

152.   Who?

Who am I? I ask.
Dust and grace, is my answer.
Who are you? I ask.

153.   Loving

God of love, love me,
without help, where would I be?
Love outshines problems.

154. Glad

I love God gladly,
He cares for me and the lost;
we'll make history.

155. Heat

The heat of healing
irradiates my body
and cold soul of fear.

156. Overcomer

I had hidden rage.
Affirmation helped me heal:
love will overcome.

157. Fountain

Never the heart dies,
or dreams to fill a big brain:
control a fountain?

158. Light Rain

Tip-tap, drips patter,
drops tapping on our rooftop:
the sky lands lightly.

159. Leaking Rain

Broken roof tiles leak,
while new rain waters farmland
ruling over us.

160.   *In Contention*

I count all I have,
counterbalancing dark thoughts:
let me live in hope.

161.   *Mop*

Mop, vacuum cleaner,
rags, polish, detergent, broom:
my mind being cleansed.

162.   *Wrapped*

Wrapped within winter,
water rushes to its rest,
ready for its time.

163. True

God, I call you true,
everything else can go skew;
I gain direction.

164. Who?

Who to trust? Who leads?
Fast running out of heroes:
who can I believe?

165. Midwinter

Thank you for birdsong
in winter, buds being born
to foretell what's new.

166. Pulse

Waterfront street band,
xylophone, saxophone, drums;
a nation's heartbeat.

167. Daily News

Daily hope is real
although challenges abound;
grace is God's to give.

168. Ladder

One hundred steps rose
into the sky, ninety-nine
or more were failures.

169. *Power Switch*

Blackout! Full moonshine.
The Sun has remembered us:
this triad works well.

170. *Shining*

Jesus shines in me
loving away all failures
lighting up my face.

171. *Misery*

Melancholic and
misanthropic, I try to
stare down misery.

172. Tea

As I boiled water
to make a cup of chai tea
a fresh haiku brewed.

173. Wonder

Wondrous is our God:
wonders of heaven and earth
unite at sunset.

174. Dim

Light in mid-winter:
a dim shroud of clouds masks us:
a cold, wet blanket.

175. Dubai

Desert dust like fog
obscures blue sky and truth
beyond tall towers.

176. Opportunity

Looking for a way?
Hard up for a true saviour?
Try Jesus, the Christ.

177. Times

These were times for me,
and lots of time lives in me:
let it tick lightly.

178. Clock

Hear it in your heart:
the clock of eternity
beats billions of years.

179. As It Turned Out

My birth was not free,
nothing was cheap or easy;
until grace was here.

180. Phony

It's a phony world,
a post-modern smorgasbord:
facades in mirrors.

181.   Mask

Each face is a mask:
a soul veiled by an ego
in a persona.

182.   Populism

Lower and lower,
closer to the world nadir:
who will lead us up?

183.   Many

I'm one in many,
finding my place in the world:
some significance.

184. Futurology

The future is caused,
blueprinting our destiny
can be realised.

185. Dark Mood

The mood of the world
is dark, it's lost its footing,
and lost its soul-peace.

186. Unfree

Dumb down media,
imprison minds in groupthink:
welcome to the West.

187. *Mathematics*

God's CV is sure,
mathematician, artist,
father of all life.

188. *Locked*

Round and round I go,
endless circles of the past,
locked inside nowhere.

189. *Bin Scrummaging*

Yes, his clothes aren't washed,
and though he smells like seaweed,
he wears holy shoes.

190.   Children of 9/11

Whispers of deep sin,
babies of our hate or love:
crucified towers.

191.   Safety

We look for safety.
The only safe place is God.
He never leaves you.

192.   Asleep

I wish I could sleep
and forget all about art
and reality.

193. *Double Cross*

Brothers betray but
Jesus accuses them not:
cancelling their debts.

194. *Day*

Just a lovely day,
the temperature of heaven:
blue sky with white wisps.

195. *Races*

Why hate someone just
because they look different,
black, brown, white, yellow?

196. On Our Journey

O, God have mercy,
we're but dust and DNA:
Good Father, guide us.

197. Relatives

Baby butterfly,
uncle tree, grandfather sun,
mother water: home.

198. Exist

Here I am alone,
my gift is my existence:
I think, I become.

199. Ahead

Keep looking ahead,
the stars are always above:
home is in your heart.

200. Hearts

Feed the hearts you love
so they find their strength to fly,
lifting mighty wings.

201. No Robbing

Bullies can't rob us
of any rights to exist
or to speak our truths.

202. Failures

All traces of wounds
from the past are washed away,
forgiving failures.

203. Okay

Don't worry, my soul,
everything will be okay:
God knows everything.

204. Robbed

Don't rob someone's voice,
conspiring in cold silence,
turning a deaf ear.

205. Who?

Who is your true friend?
Who walks down the road with you?
Who cares about you?

206. Deadly Memes

Weak race, weaker sex,
might is right, white is better;
but God is true North.

207. True Home

You are my home, God,
where on Earth was made for me,
but to be in you?

208. Proud

Trees wearing new clothes,
blue sky beams on green valleys,
pruned roses reborn.

209. Remembering '69

On Tranquillity
the fair Eagle has landed:
cosmic connection.

210. Teabags

The scent of teabags
is a pre-taste of flavours
bursting energy.

211.　*A Poo*

The cat scratched a hole,
deposited her day's dregs,
covered clean with soil.

212.　*Change of Season*

A long, cold winter,
of drab days and starless nights:
hungry for sunshine.

213.　*Press Refresh*

Stop. A day of rest.
Press refresh. Reset your brain.
Give thanks. Breathe freely.

214. Healer

Let God's grace be true,
let the Healer rule the world:
nature's laws prevail.

215. Voices

Voices loud or soft,
godfathers or gatekeepers:
quelling your spirit.

216. Energy-Matter

Thermodynamic
energy and matter merge:
formulaic world.

217. *Days of Darkness*

The world has gone dark.
Biggest lies make the most noise.
Propaganda rules.

218. *Femicide*

Don't hurt any girls.
Don't kill mother earth or wombs
or babies and hopes.

219. *Roots*

Life is like a tree.
God loves me and I love God:
my roots make me real.

220. Authentic

Authenticity.
Win, draw or lose, that is me;
don't stop being free.

221. Born to Roam

I wasn't born free,
I was born seeking my soul:
my strength born sweetly.

222. Battalions

Gas-guzzling, ugly
SUV battalions
blitz the long, grey road.

223. The Crass Times

Phony pouting mouths
and populist pretenders
sprout their vanity.

224. Birth Right

I wasn't born good,
nor made to be negative
or some neurotic.

225. Aspire

It's all good with God,
but not with society:
aspire higher.

226. *Age of Vanity*

Sanctimonious,
proud, self-righteous, self-loving
mean loud mouths abound.

227. *Egotists*

They "know" everything:
high IQ, low empathy
types who domineer.

228. *Marriage*

No blame games, baby!
No record of wrongs is kept,
faithful forever.

229. Mercy Again

Have mercy on me,
so there's mercy in my heart:
love is from above.

230. Infinity

Energy is fixed,
infinity leads to God:
horizons vanish.

231. Balance (2)

Equilibrium
is a balance of forces;
the God-force comes first.

232. Cradled

He watches my back
and steps, he cradles my heart:
his name is Yahweh.

233. Cord

Cut the cord and laugh,
unhook those who would catch you:
I move forward, free.

234. Fatigue

Dry mouth and faint voice,
tiredness overcomes me
like a long, slow curse.

235. Systems Thinking

I think about this:
we're input-output machines,
never demi-gods.

236. Surrender

Who would surrender?
God knows best how best to bless:
I give up for love.

237. Storm

Like cowering cats,
listen to the storm wind howl:
sounds worse than it looks.

238. Oxygen

Something beautiful
about the scent of mown grass:
sun-fuelled oxygen.

239. New Day

A dawn splash signals
a fresh start, recovering
in African rain.

240. Garden

We're garden beings.
Soil, animal, brains evolve:
rocket into space.

241. Cool

"Cool" is not so cool.
Only love is always cool.
Love sets my heart free.

242. Perspective

Hope is never wrong,
in the deep valley look up:
see all from the peak.

243. Why

Why am I alive?
I pledge to serve a kingdom:
You're the meaning, Lord.

244. Numbers

Orbits, DNA,
gravity, fixed speed of light:
it's a numbers game.

245. Forever God

God is good and great,
he's proven real by mercy,
living forever.

246. Orion

Line of Orion:
a procession of three kings
across the night sky.

247. Why Haiku?

In three simple lines,
insights on scraps of paper:
a strong, sharp focus.

248. Dream

Sleep enfolded me:
in my dream, I was in space,
near deathless starlight.

249. Sky

First, the sky was full.
Life confidence surged in me:
God switched my heart on.

250. Beyond Hope

What calls beyond hope?
As far as the eye can see,
Truth is always there.

251. Motion

Ever moving on,
obeying laws of motion:
my heart pumps life blood.

252. Where to Look?

Where's my happiness?
I won't find it in others:
it's within my head.

253. Fortress

This is my fortress,
where I've made peace with the world,
a Cape garden home.

254. From Distress to De-obsess

Decompress? De-stress?
No, de-obsess. Redirect:
face up to the One.

255. Made by Time

Finding my true self,
I live to see true progress:
made by Time with love.

256. Real

Not sure who to trust?
Parachute Salinger in:
detect what's phoney.

257. What Matters

All matter is made,
energy incarnated:
God forms all atoms.

258. Marriage

After thirty years,
we're still a going concern:
our home stays at peace.

259. Jobs

I do each work well:
God is indispensable,
not me or my job.

260. Love

We love and we lose,
we love and, at last, we win:
never giving in.

261. Cards

I play the cards dealt,
what I don't have, I don't have;
I'll pick an Ace soon.

262. Joshua 1:9

Faith defeats all fear,
God gives me strength to believe,
commanding courage.

263. Work

Days of laziness
pass into oblivion
but work creates hope.

264. Changes

All is change in Time,
age, appearance, conditions.
But God stays the same.

265. *Bloodflow*

My heart pumps my blood;
keep my fountain bright and fresh
so my smile prospers.

266. *Little Ones*

Love little people,
baby, toddler, child, youngster,
bless the children's hearts.

267. *Unbeliefs*

I don't believe in
skin colour, populism,
tribes, clubs, demi-gods.

268. *Hometown*

Creature of the coast,
diverse, colourful city:
African gateway.

269. *Safe*

Many lies whisper,
many memories taunt me:
yet, in God I'm safe.

270. *Country Roads*

Songs from the country,
songs of the heart brought me joy
on a shining day.

271. Contours

On the contour path
scents of fynbos fill the air,
far above rough streets.

272. Haitus

I write a poem,
the power is live in me,
off the national grid.

273. Lust

Lust living in me
is a shadow of my heart,
co-creating risks.

---

274. Bills

More days and more bills:
Is life just a dollar bill?
Money makes us mad.

275. Befriended

Be my friend, Cosmos,
at home in the universe,
nature's calm embrace.

276. Windy Day

Lungs of earth blow hard
rushing, rustling in tree tops:
thoughts swirl in my head.

277. Flow

Almighty Christ God:
from my heart a river flows
back to its full source.

278. What's Gone?

Blown away in time,
the world I was born into:
hold my last hopes, Lord.

279. Energy Flow

Fog of my mind clears,
fresh energy fills my heart:
I can hope again.

280. Believe

Let boldness guide me,
being a believing man;
let God rule my heart.

281. Hosepipe

Summer watering,
scents of heat and settling dust;
watched by early stars.

282. Test of Love

Forgiveness tests love,
only pure love can forgive,
a gift of free hearts.

283. Pledge

Gentlemen agree,
love and respect all women:
wombs nurture futures.

284. Shoreline

Salt and pepper shore
holds the emerald ocean:
white surf dissolving.

285. Open the Gates

Unlock the handcuffs,
let happiness snap the chains:
as light bursts inside.

286. Heavenly Hug

My poor prayers go out
to those whose dads broke their hearts:
may heaven hug you.

287. Small Scene in Houston

Trees, pretty as girls,
flicker in chilly sunshine:
tulips in Houston.

288. Pain Free

Let me be pain free,
body, memories, future;
remade well and whole.

289. 3-in-1

Write "faith" in my heart,
"believe" across my forehead,
then send me courage.

290. Working Life

Work to be worthy,
use your power to produce:
God is a fair boss.

291. Not Alone

God alone guides me,
He's my strongest comforter:
I'm never alone.

292. Outside

Blue day beckoning,
sky glides into my window
calling me outside.

293. Love Challenge

Who's ready to love?
What can stop all heaven's love?
Please open my heart.

294. Chrysalis

Born at dawn, I live,
states unfold, conditions grow:
let sky and I fly.

295. *Reign of the Fearful*

Boring smug old snobs
voting for a past's that's gone,
afraid of what's new.

296. *Our Times*

Monocultural
populists play tricks with truth,
exalting power.

297. *Feliz Navidad*

Think kindly, as much
as you have been forgiven:
his gift is immense.

298. *Kiss the Time*

Catch change on its way,
kiss the time as it goes by,
lightly touch the world.

299. *Rainbow of Races*

The rainbow nation
is rising together now:
Arise, Africa.

300. *Miracle of Light*

Light's the fastest thing,
physics founded on photons:
power without mass.

301. Reactionary

Only narrow minds
see the world as theirs to own,
clutching privilege.

302. The Stubborn Optimist

Just had a nightmare.
So I must have been asleep:
beats being sleepless.

303. The Tall Walk

Walk in the strong call,
feel tall in grace, given free,
be bold in spirit.

304. When Giants Fall

Opponents line up,
giants with javelins face us:
be my strength and aim.

305. Not Impossible

Not impossible
is your dream of excellence;
trust the possible.

306. New Times

Let's set sail again,
be Captain of my journey,
be Guide of my path.

307. *No More Aloneness*

No hate: love has won.
No fear: faith has overcome.
No room for self-doubt.

308. *No Fear*

No fear of failure
holds me back from my mission:
to be the best me.

309. *Ending*

Death I've seen somewhere
and God is there, everywhere:
heaven's gate opened.

310. Nocturne

Night skies are sparkling,
Southern Cross arches the sea:
creation rises.

311. Location

My soul home I made
south in untamed Africa:
infinite Cape Town.

312. Walls

Berlin's wall is down.
When will Israel's wall fall?
When love wins the peace.

313. True Beauty

A beautiful face
can be in any colour;
paint my heart blood red.

314. The Champion

Love is champion,
kindness crushing bitterness:
aspiring high.

315. Template

Universal man:
no retreat into your skin,
no death for our souls.

316. *Abundance*

When will this rain end?
When the dams are full, I heard,
groundwater swelling.

317. *Stay free*

Spring all your strong traps:
don't let old dreams and nightmares
grip and smother you.

318. *Imagination*

Imagination
is to think with no boxes
in the Universe.

---

319. Formula

Let faith replace fear,
let love overcome hatred:
peace ruling each day.

320. Forever

Now, as in the past,
God is the God of science:
nature's timeless rules.

321. Blessed

A pain-free body
and mind: is this a real dream
or my redemption?

THE END

About the Author

Michael J. Lee, Master of Philosophy (Futures Studies) (cum laude), Master of Arts in English, Honours-Baccalaureus Theologiae (cum laude), Higher Education Diploma (with distinction).

Michael enjoys reading, writing, painting, sketching, jogging and watching powerful movies, having built up a private collection of several hundred DVDs and Blu-ray films spanning the entire history of cinema to the present. He has been married to Sannettha since 1990 and the couple have two daughters, Michaela, a food and cosmetic scientist, and Melissa, a linguist and business analyst.

Lee has been CEO of the ATM Industry Association (www.atmia. com), which has over 11,000 members in about 70 countries, since 2005. He is chairperson of the Consortium for Next Gen ATMs which has over 400 companies participating in this future-proofing exercise to link over 3 million ATMs with more than 5 billion mobile phones.

Michael is a qualified futurist, artist and writer living in Cape Town. In 2015, he published *Heartbeat*, a documentary novel about the world's first human heart transplant. His two works about understanding the social future through interdisciplinary causal analysis are *Knowing our Future* and *Codebreaking our Future*, both available on Amazon.com.

He has written two science fiction works, *Chrysalis*, a story about the world's first head transplant, and *Earthrise 2036*, a part-documentary, part-imaginary journey through the evolution of humanity from the rawest of origins in the Cradle of Humankind to the age of space exploration.

TITLES BY THE AUTHOR

SCIENCE FICTION

Chrysalis: A surgical sci-fi story about immortal potential

Earthrise 2036

DOCUMENTARY NOVEL

Heartbeat

POEMS

Three Hundred and Twenty-One Haiku

Not Yet in Heaven

Rebirths

PLAYS

The Archive - a play about the last days of Friedrich Nietzsche

NON-FICTION

Passage to Faith

A New Logic For Faith

The Courage to Believe

FUTURE STUDIES

Codebreaking our Future

Knowing our Future

www.beyondheads.com
www.michaeljlee.com
michael@positivedestiny.org

---

www.ingramcontent.com/pod-product-compliance
Lightning Source LLC
Chambersburg PA
CBHW022104050726

47591CB00002B/666